You Can Be an Amazing Friend!

John Pritchett

Library of Congress Control Number: 2023922194

Copyright © 2023 John Pritchett

All rights reserved. This book or any portion thereof may not be reproduced or used in any manner whatsoever without the express written permission of the publisher, except for the use of brief quotations in a book review.

Published on Amazon by John Pritchett

Dedicated to my best friend Dawn.

Other books by John Pritchett.

You Can Be a Hero Too!

Chapter One

Making Friends

Hey friend! Making friends is like finding a treasure chest of happiness. Friends bring us joy, comfort, and support—pretty amazing, right? Being a friend is like being a superhero, and anyone can be one!

To be the best friend ever, let's learn about cool qualities. Like trust—keeping secrets safe, honesty—telling the truth, and keeping promises—being a promise-keeper. It's like unlocking the code to friendship magic!

In this book, we're going to have a blast learning about these special qualities. It's like a guidebook on how to be the coolest friend on the block. So, buckle up, because we're on a journey to discover the secrets of being an amazing friend!

Chapter Two

Trust

Imagine trust as the super firm foundation of a friendship house. Trust helps us build awesome relationships with our buddies. It's like believing in them to be honest, and loyal. Trustworthy pals tell the truth, keep promises, and care about our feelings. It's like the magical glue that keeps friends close.

Now, think of trust like a special jar. Every time you do something awesome for a friend, like sharing a secret or standing up for a friend, you add marbles to the jar. The more marbles, the more your friends trust you. But, if you do something not-so-cool, like lying or breaking promises, you take marbles out. The fewer marbles you have, the less your friends trust you. Filling the jar is tough, but emptying it is super easy.

Trust is something you can only do with someone whose jar is filled up, not emptied. Even though you can't see or touch trust, you can totally feel it and show it. It's like a gift you share with friends. Trust is a skill you can practice and get better at. Every day, you build trust, you make life way better. Trust is like a super awesome invisible treasure!

Chapter Three

Being Honest

Being honest is like being a superhero of trust. Friends are like sidekicks, and superheroes are always honest with their pals. Honesty is like having a superpower that means telling the truth and doing what's right. It's not pretending your brother ate the last cookie when you did. Being honest is like building a trust and respect fortress. It's not always easy, but it's the secret to making life awesome and having the best friendships.

Trust is like a friendship treasure, and honesty is the key to finding it. Friends are like partners on a treasure hunt, and honesty has two cool parts: speaking truthfully and acting truthfully.

Speaking truthfully is like using your truth power. For example, if you ate the last cookie, you don't say your brother did. That's like using a lie, and friends don't lie.

Acting truthfully is like doing the right thing. For example, if you find a wallet on the street, you don't keep it. That's like stealing, and friends don't steal. You should try to give the wallet back to its owner or find an adult who can help.

Honesty is like the magic potion that makes trust and respect grow. When you're honest, friends know they can count on you. But if you're not honest, trust and respect shrink, and you might get into trouble or lose your sidekicks.

Being honest might feel hard, but it's the coolest choice. Sometimes you might want to use a little fib, but honesty is like winning a superhero trophy because it makes you feel awesome and helps you have the best friendships ever.

Being an honesty superhero takes practice. You have to decide to be honest in everything, even the small stuff. Think before you speak or act. Always tell the truth, even if it feels tough.

Being honest is like a skill you practice. You have to choose to be honest in everything, even the small stuff. Before you speak or do something, think about whether it's true and right. Always tell the truth, even when it's hard, and try not to exaggerate or bend the truth. That way, you'll become really good at being honest, and it will make your life better!

Chapter Four

Keeping Promises

Promises between friends are like secret handshakes - super important! They show you care about each other and want to be the best pals. When you promise something, it's like making a cool friendship pact. The golden rule: if you promise, you gotta keep it! That means doing what you said you would do. Keeping promises is like earning a superhero badge of trust. But hey, if something comes up and you can't keep your promise, just tell your friend and say sorry. It's okay; we're all learning how to be great friends.

Imagine promises as friendship glue. They make your bond strong and unbreakable. Do you have a friend who always keeps their promises to you? That's like having a super reliable teammate in the friendship league!

A promise is like saying, "I pinky swear I'll do this" or "I won't do that." It's serious business. When you make a promise, be a promise-keeper. That means doing what you said or not doing what you promised not to do. Keeping promises shows you're the real deal - someone friends can trust. It's like having a secret power that makes your friendship awesome.

Sometimes, keeping promises can be tricky. Life happens, and you might forget or face challenges. But even then, try your best or tell your friend why you can't keep your promise. Say sorry and ask for forgiveness - friends understand.

Breaking a promise is like dropping an ice cream cone - it's a bummer. It can make your friend feel sad or mad. Plus, it can mess up your friendship vibe. So, be careful about the promises you make. If you can't keep a promise, spill the beans to your friend ASAP.

Want to become a promise-keeping pro? Here's the game plan: think before you promise, make sure you can do it, and don't promise too much. Writing promises down is like having a superhero journal - it helps you remember and keeps you on track.

Building the promise-keeping habit takes time, like leveling up in a video game. It might be a bit of work, but it's worth it. Being a friend means keeping your promises and being someone your pals can always count on. So, promise away and be the best friend ever!

Chapter Five

Consistency

Consistency is like having a superhero power! It means doing things the same way every time, like showing up for basketball practice on time, every day. It's like a trust-building high-five between friends. Imagine if your friend always changed the game rules - that would be confusing! So, being consistent in important stuff helps your friends rely on you, like when you keep your promises.

Consistency is like having a superhero routine that makes you more reliable and trustworthy. When you're consistent, you can feel proud of your awesome self and the cool things you achieve.

Being consistent doesn't mean you can't try new stuff. You can still try new things and be a creative genius. But for important stuff, like keeping promises, sticking to the plan helps everyone.

Know what's important to you, and it's like having a treasure map. Others can understand your actions better. Creating routines is like having a superhero schedule. For example, if you visit your best friend every Saturday, they'll know to expect it and appreciate your focus on them.

Now, imagine you promise to help your friend build a model airplane. That's a big promise! But guess what? You can break it into smaller, doable steps. Like one Saturday, help choose the model kit. The next, gather tools and materials. The Saturdays after that assist with cutting, gluing, painting, and adding stickers. Once it's done, enjoy the toy model together!

Being consistent isn't always a piece of cake. To make it easier, be realistic about what you can do. If helping every Saturday is too much, maybe offer to help with picking the model. Write your promises on a calendar and share them with your family so they can be your sidekicks in keeping your word.

Sometimes, you might promise more than you can do. It happens! Learn from those times and figure out why. Did you promise too much or forget because you didn't write it down? Understanding your superhero promises helps you be more consistent in the future. Remember, consistency is a habit you can grow and make super strong!

# Chapter Six
Gossip and Rumors

Gossip and rumors can be like sneaky little monsters that try to hurt friendships. They're words that might not be true and can make people feel sad or embarrassed. Imagine if someone spread stories about you—it wouldn't feel good, right? So, when you hear gossip, you have the power to stop it!

Gossip and rumors can really mess up friendships. They're like words people say or write that might not be true. Sometimes, folks do it because they're bored, curious, jealous, or angry. But here's the scoop: gossip and rumors hurt the feelings of the people they're about, and even the ones who spread them.

Check out these examples:

- Gossip: "Did you hear Lisa got a new bike for her birthday? I bet she didn't even say thank you to her parents."

- Rumor: "I heard Jake cheated on his math test. He copied the answers from Sam's paper."

Gossip and rumors aren't cool because they can make the person being talked about feel sad or embarrassed. And guess what? They also make the person spreading them look mean, dishonest, or not trustworthy.

But hey, you're not powerless! If you hear or see gossip, you can choose what to do. You can pretend you didn't hear it—change the subject, walk away, or focus on something else. This way, you don't give gossip any attention.

If you're feeling bold, you can also tell the person spreading gossip or rumors that it's not cool. Say something like, "That's not nice to say about someone. Please stop," or "I don't know if that's true, and I don't want to spread it.

Remember, gossip and rumors aren't the way to go. They can hurt people and mess up your own friendships. Instead, try being kind, honest, and respectful to everyone. That's the secret to making positive connections and building trust with others.

Chapter Seven
Mistakes and Apologies

Hey there! We all goof up sometimes—it's totally normal. When you mess up or let someone down, it's cool to own up to it and make things right.

Making a good apology is like being a friendship superhero. It's not just saying "I'm sorry," but also explaining why, promising not to do it again, and making up for it. It's a skill that helps fix things and shows you care about your friend's feelings.

To make a super apology, think about what went wrong and how your friend feels. For instance, if you broke their toy, think about how bummed or mad they might be.

Then, find a good time and place to say sorry. Don't wait too long or hide from your friend. Pick a quiet spot where you can talk without interruptions.

Look your friend in the eyes and talk in a calm and respectful voice. No excuses or blaming others! Be honest and humble. Say, "I'm sorry" and admit what you did, like, "I'm sorry I broke your toy. I shouldn't have played with it without asking."

Explain why you did it and promise not to do it again. Like, "I was curious about how it worked, but I should have asked. Next time, I'll follow the rules."

Ask for forgiveness and offer to make things right. Say, "Can you forgive me? I'll save up my allowance and get you a new toy."

Listen to what your friend says and respect their feelings. They might need some time, and that's okay. Don't bug them or expect forgiveness right away. Thank them for listening and showing you care.

Making a good apology might be tough, but it helps you feel better and makes your friendship even stronger. Remember, everyone messes up, but what matters is learning from it and being awesome to your friends!

Chapter Eight

Talking & Listening

Hey! Talking with friends is like having a secret code for awesome friendships. It's super important to be honest and open when you chat with your pals. Imagine if you had to keep everything to yourself—it wouldn't be much fun, right? So, let's learn the secrets of great communication!

Encourage your friends to share their thoughts and feelings with you. It's like creating a cool zone where everyone can talk freely. Open communication is like having a treasure map for building strong and healthy friendships. It's all about being honest, clear, and willing to talk about thoughts, feelings, and concerns in a friendly way.

Sometimes, talking with friends can get a bit emotional. It's totally okay! Manage your emotions by taking a break if you need to. If your friend gives you feedback, don't get all defensive. Try to understand what they're saying—it's like they're sharing a super valuable gift with you.

Feedback is when someone tells you how you did on something, like a drawing or a school project, or something you didn't do, like keeping a promise. They can say what they liked or didn't like and maybe give you ideas to make it even better next time. It's like when your friend says, "I like how you used lots of colors, but maybe you can add more details to the trees."

Feedback is useful because it helps you learn and get better at things. So, when someone gives you feedback, it's good to listen and think about how you can use it to improve what you're doing. Being honest is a must in communication. Tell the truth about what you think and feel. No hiding stuff or being tricky. And here's a cool tip: let your friends know that you're cool with them giving you feedback. Say you value their thoughts and feelings. It's like planting a seed for super strong friendships.

Remember, feedback from friends is like a growth potion. It might be tough to hear, but it's a sign they care about you and want to help you become an even more awesome person. So, let's unlock the secret code of honest and open communication and grow together!

Hey friend! Listening is like having a superhero power for making awesome friendships. It shows you care, respect, and understand your buddies. Imagine if no one listened—it would be like talking to a wall! So, being a good listener is key to being an amazing friend.

Listening might seem like a little work, but it's super worth it. Your friends will think you're the best listener ever, and you'll learn so much about them. Plus, it helps you solve problems and have a blast together.

When your friends talk, give them your full attention. No distractions! Nod, keep eye contact, and use cool facial expressions to show you're really into what they're saying.

Don't interrupt, even if you have something awesome to share. Let them finish, and then it's your turn. Ask questions that help you understand better or clear up any confusion you might have. It's like giving your friends a friendship spotlight.

Once they're done, show them you were listening by repeating a little bit of what they said. You could say, for example, if they were telling you about a camping trip, you could say, "Wow! It sounds like you had a really cool time.

Then you could ask cool little open-ended questions. These questions are the ones that start with words like what, how, why, where, when, who, or which. They're like magic keys that open up richer and cooler conversations. Getting back to camping, you could ask: 'What did you like most about camping?" Or "How did you make a fire?

Here's a tip for being a super listener: don't jump to solutions. If your friend's talking about a problem, imagine how they feel and resist the urge to be a superhero fixer. Sometimes, they just need a friendly ear.

Another tip for being a super listener is to be patient! Some friends take more time to express themselves, so give them the time they need. Listening is like a cool skill you can practice and get better at. The more you do it, the more awesome a friend you become. So, let's listen and be the best buddies ever!

Chapter Nine

Reflection

Hey there! Growing as a friend is like going on an awesome adventure. You know what makes it even more exciting? Reflecting on your adventures and seeking feedback from friends and mentors. It's like leveling up in a video game!

Imagine you're playing baseball, and you want to get better at hitting the ball. You try, your coach gives you feedback, and then you try again until you become a hitting champ. For self-reflection, you're your own coach! You take time to think about your day and how you can be an even more fantastic friend.

To start this cool habit, find a quiet spot each day, like before bedtime or after school. It could be in your room, a park, or any quiet place where you can focus. It's like having your own thinking corner!

Journaling is another awesome way to reflect. Write down your thoughts, experiences, and reflections. It's like making a map of your feelings. Ask yourself questions like "What did I learn today?" or "How did I handle that situation?" It helps you figure out what went well, what could be improved, and what challenges you faced.

During this reflection time, explore your feelings. Pay attention to why you feel happy or sad. It's like being a detective, finding out the causes of your emotions.

And don't forget to celebrate your victories, no matter how small! Maybe you made a new friend or aced a tricky homework problem. Recognizing your successes makes you feel awesome!

Now, mistakes happen—no biggie! Treat them like a chance to grow. Reflect on what went wrong and think about how you can do better next time. It's like turning oops moments into opportunities!

Reflecting on past goals and setting new ones is super fun. What do you want to achieve, and how can you make it happen? It's like having your own personal treasure map for success!

So, let's reflect, celebrate, learn from oopsies, and set new goals. You're on your way to becoming the best friend ever!

Reflecting on our adventures helps us grow as friends, just like leveling up in a video game. So, let's continue this exciting adventure, be the best buddies ever, and make every day filled with friendship magic!

Chapter Ten

You Can Be an Amazing Friend!

Congratulations, awesome friend! You've completed the friendship adventure! In Chapter One, we learned that making friends is like finding a treasure chest of happiness, and everyone can be a superhero friend. Trust, honesty, and keeping promises are the secret codes to friendship magic.

Trust, our super firm foundation, was explored in Chapter Two. Trust is like an invisible jar where we add marbles by doing awesome things for friends. It's a super awesome invisible treasure!

Chapter Three turned us into honesty superheroes. Speaking truthfully and acting truthfully are the key ingredients to finding friendship treasure. Being an honesty superhero takes practice and feels like winning a superhero trophy!

In Chapter Four, we mastered the art of keeping promises, secret handshakes between pals. Promises are like a friendship glue that strengthens our bond. Thinking before promising and keeping a superhero journal help us become promise-keeping pros!

Consistency, our superhero power from Chapter Five, involves doing things the same way every time. It builds trust and reliability, like having a superhero routine. Consistency is a habit we can grow and make super strong.

Chapter Six warned us about gossip and rumors, the sneaky monsters that can hurt friendships. Instead of spreading or believing gossip, we choose kindness, honesty, and respect, building positive connections and trust.

In Chapter Seven, we embraced mistakes and apologies. Making a good apology is like being a friendship superhero, involving saying sorry, explaining why, promising not to do it again, and making up for it.

Chapter Eight revealed the secrets of talking & listening. Open communication and being a good listener are crucial for strong and healthy friendships. Feedback from friends is like a growth potion, helping us learn and improve.

Finally, Chapter Nine explored reflection, the exciting adventure of growing as friends. Reflecting on our adventures, celebrating victories, learning from mistakes, and setting new goals make every day an exciting journey filled with friendship magic!

You've unlocked the secrets of being an amazing friend. Keep practicing these skills, and you'll continue to be the most amazing friend ever! Remember, every day is a new opportunity for friendship magic!

Made in the USA
Columbia, SC
17 January 2024